A BOOK OF DEVOTIONAL READINGS

Life is a Metaphor

Recognizing God in the Everyday

Denise Larson Cooper

ROCKFORD, ILLINOIS

ISBN-13: 978-0692403440
ISBN-10: 0692403442

Cover Photo © Denise Larson Cooper

Book Layout © 2014 BookDesignTemplates.com

Life is a Metaphor/ Denise Larson Cooper. — 1st ed.

To my family and friends who have listened to me talk about writing a book for the past ten years. Finally we can talk about something else.

CONTENTS

How to Use this Book

During His earthly ministry, Jesus taught people using parables, similes and metaphors. This book of devotional readings was written to help people today see how Jesus, through the Holy Spirit, still uses metaphors to teach us about God, sin and His everlasting kingdom. It is my prayer that readers will hear Jesus speaking metaphorically in their daily lives so their understanding of God in Christ will grow deeper and their faith in the Lord will grow stronger.

The Bible translation used in the citations is the 1984 New International Version (NIV) unless otherwise stated: English Standard Version (ESV); Holman Christian Standard Bible (HCSB); International Standard Version (ISV); King James Version (KJV); New Living Translation (NLT).

{ 1 }

Long Range

In the gymnastics community, athletes are training hard for the Summer Olympics. For those gymnasts who have a shot at the Games, their dream is upon them. Positioned to represent the USA, these girls are the survivors and the strivers, the ones who entered the sport expecting to cut an Olympic path and who have finally risen from the ranks of thousands to come so close to the prize. However, for all but these few, the path has grown too steep and too demanding. Many start the journey but obstacles—the fear of failure, the coaches' demands, or the exhaustion of intense workouts—overpower these girls, and their dreams die. Some simply grow tired of the chase, or they fall to injury.

The elite few, however, can't rest on their laurels yet: They still face thousands of hours of work and preparation for the Olympic trials. Throughout the grueling hours ahead, each girl must cling to her vision. As the days pass and the possibilities for making the team increase, the coaches and athletes must become more united in mind and purpose. Only by working together as a single unit can the dream become a reality.

Here's the metaphor:

We need to focus on the long-range vision of heaven. Our goal in this life should be the eternal kingdom of God. The pursuit of eternity begins in the daily moments of this temporal life. Our faith in Christ calls us onto the path of sanctification, on which we are made holy through the power of the Holy Spirit and on which we are made new creations in Christ. It is a demanding path, and the pitfalls can prove to be overwhelming as we struggle with our sinful nature and against the power of Satan. Many reject its demands: Some will be deceived by falsehoods, while others will be mesmerized by the life of sin and its temporal rewards and remain blinded to God's truth.

For Christians, the long range goal of heaven means entering into a life of service to our neighbor—anyone whom Christ puts onto our path. Our service should be given freely each day in the name of Jesus Christ. At times, however, we see this service as burdensome, but when we remind ourselves of the finished work of Christ on our behalf, we can serve others out of love for Christ. By His love we are united with Him in His ministry. Christ calls us to unite with Him in heart and mind through the power of the Holy Spirit, to live according to His commandments: Love God with all your heart, and love your neighbor as [you do] yourself.

Many days we grow weary on the path. We despair and lose sight of the goal. We get distracted by sin and then doubt the Word of God. Sometimes our hope wanes. But we shouldn't give up: We should power up! God has given us the means to carry on. Let us augment our spiritual life through reading and memorizing Scripture and rising early for time alone with God in prayer, singing songs of praise to our Savior, listening for the prompting of the Spirit, and encouraging others along the path of holiness. Perhaps above all, we should participate in corporate worship, where we hear God's Word preached and where we celebrate Holy Communion, the means of grace and spiritual nourishment on the path to holiness.

Paul said, "For physical training is of some value, but godliness has value for all things, holding promise for both the present life and the life to come" (1 Timothy 4:8).

To "run and not grow weary . . . and walk and not faint" (Isaiah 40:31), we have to live in holiness and righteousness through our Lord and Savior. He unites us to His holy, righteous life by the power of the Holy Spirit, so the Kingdom of God is our future reality.

{ 2 }

Maturity

I had an interesting conversation recently with another coach. He noted, insightfully I thought, that the difference between successful athletes and those unsuccessful in achieving their goals or pushing through struggles was their level of maturity.

This perspective opened my eyes. I spend many days staring into the faces of crying gymnasts and telling them, in effect, to stop crying and grow up. Now I see that their crying is connected to their immaturity: They have not matured enough as athletes in the sport to accept constructive criticism about their efforts. In effect, when I tell them to grow up, I am asking them to develop their minds and bodies for the sport. Of course, helping them to mature takes much patience on my part. It takes a long time for an athlete to mature.

The time it takes to mature is different for each athlete; however, some stubbornly refuse to grow. In the case of a gymnast's obstinacy, discipline has to be administered and hard lines drawn if she is going to develop her potential fully.

Here's the metaphor:

God expects us to mature in our faith. Hebrews 6:1 says, "Therefore let us leave the elementary teachings about Christ and go on to maturity."

In the early stages of faith, we have a nominal understanding of Christ's love for us. We have heard that He died for us, perhaps not understanding the fullness of His sacrifice. In our immaturity, we use that knowledge to try to persuade Him to do things for us. We treat Him as a benevolent uncle or Santa Claus, giving Him a list of things we want or think we need. How do we grow out of this immature thinking and move forward into a more fully developed faith in Christ? We must turn to the power of the Holy Spirit.

To mature in faith means to conform to Christ through the power of the Holy Spirit. Paul gives us these simple directions for becoming mature Christians. "Be joyful. Grow to maturity, be of one mind, live in peace. And the God of love and peace will be with you" (2 Corinthians 13:11 NLT).

As we develop in faith—through fellowship with other believers, daily Scripture reading and study and prayer—our minds focus on Christ, and we become more conformed to Him. We also begin to recognize when we are being immature and arguing every little thing with God. We begin to accept the trials that God gives us, those experiences He uses to teach us about living in Christ. We begin to receive His discipline, knowing it brings us to maturity. As we mature, we settle down, and the presence of God in Christ, His love and peace, can begin to dominate our lives. Of course, all of this maturity may come with many steps backward. This process ends only when Christ decides to call us to our eternal home.

Maturity: God's way is the only way to grow.

{ 3 }

Independence

As a friend and I were talking about her daughter, it became apparent that the girl was going through what I call "the change." This young lady was transforming from a dependent child into an independent adult.

Inevitably our happy little children become surly, emotional teenagers, convinced that our love for them has soured because of the demands that we place upon them. Simple rules that they once obeyed without question become flashpoints. In their eyes we become despots determined to ruin their lives. Homes become battle grounds, and the bomb shells of shouting, arguing and bickering drop daily as our children insist upon asserting their independence. Rebellions against the established household rules become frequent. Revolutions are fought against parents' standing in the way of their once-compliant children's new-found sense of self-reliance. What we see as disobedience in the short term brings forth a new adult—children are still disobedient, but we accept this as a rite of passage.

Still our parental love remains steadfast during these uprisings and rebellions. We acknowledge that it's a necessary phase, and we pray that, when our children's separation is completed and independence secured, our children will return to us.

Here's the metaphor:

Sin convinces us to assert our independence from God. It tells us to establish our own laws of self-rule. So we set our face against God. We question His existence, reject His Son, repudiate the Spirit, renounce the resurrection and scoff at heaven. We run boldly into the world, denouncing God and exerting our independence.

In spite of our disobedience, God's love remains steadfast. "For the Lord is good and His love endures forever; His faithfulness continues through all generations" (Psalm 100:5). Regardless of our wanton attitudes and deviant behavior, God persists in love and faithfulness. His response to us is based on who He is, a merciful loving Father, not what we do.

God sent His own Son into the world to show us who He is and to expose what we have done. He came not to condemn us for our sin, but to bring relief from the burden it places upon us. On the cross Jesus defeated sin's insurrection and ended our separation from God. The Holy Spirit lives in the world not only to illuminate our sinfulness but also to reveal God's faithfulness so we will desire to surrender our independence, which separates us from Him, and return to God's presence.

"For I am convinced that neither death nor life, neither angels nor demons, neither the present nor the future, nor any powers, neither height nor depth, nor anything else in all creation, will be able to separate us from the love of God that is in Christ Jesus our Lord" (Romans 8:38-39).

{ 4 }

Shifting Focus

My friend trains hard and competes even harder as a triathlon athlete. She has pushed her body beyond its limits, worked through excruciating pain, and finished races on the verge of collapse. She seems fearless. Yet after we took a recent bike ride in a downpour, I was surprised when she admitted a reluctance to ride in the rain. Her lack of confidence stemmed from a nasty fall that she had taken once while riding in the rain. Though afraid, she decided to ride anyway, and then something happened that she hadn't anticipated: As she and I rode through the sheets of rain together, she started to regain confidence. Talking together as we rode caused her to shift her focus from thinking about falling to following me. By the time that we arrived back at the car, her confidence had been restored.

Her renewed confidence happened when she took the focus off falling: At that point, her mind relaxed, and she was able to ride unhindered by thoughts of the past.

Here's the metaphor:

We all took a nasty fall from grace, and our sinfulness caused us to live in fear of God. The guilt we feel causes us to go through our days listing our transgressions and iniquities, all the while terrified of condemnation. We know we are sinful, but instead of confessing our sin and clinging to the saving work of Christ on the cross, we stare at our sinful nature, as though staring at it will somehow excuse it.

The sinful nature fixates on sin and rejects any interference from the Holy Spirit to root out corruption. Our sinful nature focuses on sin, celebrating our disobedience as heroism against law-abiding God; yet all the while we are fearful of God's wrath, knowing that it is the just and proper recourse against sin.

Shift your focus.

Yes, we "all have sinned and fall short of the glory of God" (Romans 3:23). However, stop staring at sin and start seeing the glory of God in Jesus Christ. Once the Savior enters your life, stare at Him. Look at Him from all sides: His earthly ministry, His crucifixion, His resurrection, and His divine life. Look at His obedience to God's law on our behalf. Then, follow Him.

When sin is the object of our thoughts, we see the depths of our sin; when Jesus is the object of our thoughts, we see the depths of God. When we feel the weight of sin upon us, we should confess it immediately and repent, which restores our commitment to follow Christ.

Regain your confidence in the Savior and all that He has done for you. Confidence in Christ lifts us from the muck and mire of sin and gives us a view of our glorious God. "So do not throw away your confidence; it will be richly rewarded" (Hebrews 10:35).

{ 5 }

The Child at Home

I always keep my hair conditioner in the same place in the shower. Yesterday as I rinsed shampoo from my hair, I reached to that spot, but it was gone. This is not the first time my conditioner has gone missing. In fact, it grows legs and walks into my girls' bathroom every time my younger daughter returns home from college.

Now, I am willing to share so long as the bottle is returned to my shower. Unfortunately, that never happens. So to avoid this situation, I bought her a bottle of conditioner when we were together at the store. That made the empty space in my shower much more irritating. I wanted to be mad. Oh, how I wanted to be mad. But, I quickly changed my perspective. Now that empty space in the shower where my conditioner belongs means that my daughter is home.

Here is the metaphor:

On Easter Sunday morning, we gather with the living God to look at the empty tomb, where the body of His Son should be. God invites us to celebrate the empty tomb because it means His Son is home.

It was a long journey back for the Son. For three days, the Light of the world was captive to the dark. "That day [was] a day of wrath, a day of distress and anguish, a day of trouble and ruin, a day of darkness and gloom, a day of clouds and blackness" (Zephaniah 1:15). During His torment in "the heart of the earth" (Matthew 12:40), He walked where sinners should have walked, because we were the ones who had "sinned against the Lord" (Deuteronomy 9:16).

But God did not "abandon [His Son] to the grave nor . . . let [His] Holy One see decay" (Psalm 16:10). Instead, Almighty God, "with a strong hand and an outstretched arm" (Deuteronomy 26:8), brought the Son out of the land of darkness and death.

Oh how glorious the empty tomb looks to God. The Light of the world shines in the Father's eyes and fills the heavenly places and all the earth. The darkness that had attempted to snuff out the Light has been overcome. "The light shines in the darkness, and the darkness has not overcome it" (John 1:5). His Son lives. "His father saw him and was filled with compassion for him; he ran to his son, threw his arms around him and kissed him." (Luke 15:20) His son "was dead and is alive again" (Luke 15:32).

The tomb is empty. The Son is home. God's heart is full.

{ 6 }

Plain Language

Gymnastics has a unique vocabulary and jargon. When I first entered the sport, I was confused by so much of what I heard that listening to coaches' talk caused my eyes to glaze over and my brain to short circuit. I couldn't make sense of conversations because of my limited knowledge and understanding of the sport.

Added to that confusion was my ignorance of the policies, procedures and protocols governing the system. In the early days, I would miss shortcuts that might have helped my athletes' ascent through the gymnastic levels. There were even a few missed camps and banquets, because I lacked the personal connections; I hadn't built sufficient inroads into the larger gymnastics community.

At last I caught on: I had learned enough vocabulary, gained coaching experience and honed my understanding of the sport.

But I still lacked something that I couldn't teach myself. I needed a mentor. Finally, a generous coach, one who had walked in this world for years, brought it all together for me. Through her eyes, I was able to see the way plainly and clearly. She patiently explained the elite requirements, outlined the difficulty and value of certain skills, and helped me understand how to put the necessary skills into a routine for my gymnasts.

Here's the metaphor:

Christianity has a unique vocabulary and jargon that can be perplexing for people who are interested in finding out more about Jesus Christ. In fact, many of the theological terms befuddle even the faithful. Some important Christian terms seem suited for use only in scholarly circles among theologians. When most of us hear words such as *justification, sanctification, incarnation* and *redemption,* we might feel lost and misdirected. However, these words should not be stumbling blocks; they are important for understanding God and the depth of His commitment to us. Yet, we often find that we trip over them in our pursuit of God in Christ. We want the pathway to God to suit us.

God is straightforward. He speaks one word above all to us, *Jesus.* "The Word became flesh and made His dwelling among us" (John 1:14). Let's put it this way: Jesus is God for dummies. Jesus came into the world so the complexities of God would be made simple. Working in unison with the Holy Spirit and Scripture, Jesus Christ is the patient guide who can lead us into all truth. He IS the revelation of God, "full of grace and truth" (John 1:14).

The Spirit of truth guides us into a deeper understanding of Jesus Christ. As we open ourselves to the Spirit through Scripture, the teachings of Christ will become plain and clear in our lives.

Jesus Christ became a man and walked in this world so that through His perfect life He would be God's perfect sacrifice for atonement. When we accept Christ's sacrifice, He unlocks the mysteries of God and shows us the pathway to eternal life.

{ 7 }

Seeing the Unseen

When she was growing up, my daughter had an imaginary friend named Zach. He was a frequent guest for dinner and play time. She would even take Zach along to other friends' homes to play.

One afternoon we all went to play at Ben's house. Ben preferred toys to imaginary friends. He owned a fleet of motorized cars. His backyard was better stocked than most parks, with swings, sandbox, a swimming pool and other accessories. On one particular day my daughter wanted to play with Zach, while Ben was interested in the sandbox. Suddenly my daughter started yelling, and then she burst into tears. Her anger was directed at Ben. Apparently an empty swing, swaying back and forth, was somehow responsible for the outburst.

As I decoded my daughter's sobs and broken sentences, I finally managed to understand: Ben had pushed Zach off the swing. Convinced that Ben had caused Zach injury, she insisted that we go home, evidence that Zach was very real to my daughter. Of course, she refused to play with anyone who treated him badly.

Here is the metaphor:

Little children have a tremendous potential for "seeing" the unseen. Jesus said, "I tell you the truth, anyone who will not receive the kingdom of God like a little child will never enter it" (Mark 10:15). For many children there is no distinction between the world that adults see and the world that they imagine: Children perceive both as real. In this verse, Jesus is insisting that we exercise our childlike ability to "see" the unseen. Jesus is saying to exercise faith. Faith gives us the capacity to "see" the "unseen" world of God's heavenly kingdom.

According to Hebrews 11:1, "Faith is being sure of what we hope for and certain of what we do not see." The Holy Spirit confirms the sure work of Christ's saving grace on the cross and makes certain that we "see" the risen Jesus ascend to His heavenly throne.

Christ's ascension to His heavenly throne comes only as a result of His resurrection. Yet, His resurrection is often a stumbling block to faith. Thomas stumbled. He insisted that "unless I see ... I will never believe" (John 20:25 ESV). Jesus showed Him the scars of His crucifixion.

To lean on the "seen" and refute the "unseen" is to lean on our own understanding and deny the wisdom of God. We need to call out to the Spirit and ask for the eyes of faith. By the

Spirit we will receive eyes to see the nail marks, a heart to understand the truth of the empty tomb, and a mind to know the Risen Lord. It is the Spirit of Christ that will broaden our faith and expand our vision to "see" the kingdom of God.

Ask the Spirit to give you the eyes of a child so by faith you will "see" our resurrected Lord in all His glory in God's eternal kingdom and study the Scriptures through the eyes of faith.

{ 8 }

The Thunder's Mouth

Occasionally a thunderstorm has been my alarm clock. Gentle peals of thunder, lightning flashes, and raindrops pinging off my bedroom window have roused me from sleep.

Thunderstorms come in a variety of intensities. Some roar through with violent intentions. I've watched lightning spears stab the ground and the wind shear branches from trees. In others, the thunder starts, its booming voice shaking the house and echoing through the heavens. Sometimes pelting rain takes center stage, riding the wind into open windows.

These storms have common features: wind, rain, thunder and lightning. Storms arise apparently from a certain combination of heat and cold, seemingly at random. But a storm does seem to have a purpose, to be timed perfectly to demonstrate the power of Nature. This power draws me to the windows to watch these mighty elements toss the clouds and pound the earth. Strangely, storms are a source of assurance and comfort to me.

Here is the metaphor:

God is three distinct persons: Father, Son and Spirit working together to demonstrate the saving power of the Almighty.

Each person is distinct, yet, in the holy essence of God, Each reveals the truth of salvation to the world. "In the beginning" (Genesis 1:1) the Father revealed the truth of redemption through creation, Israel and the promise of a Savior. When the time was right the Father introduced His Son to the world in the person of Jesus Christ. And when His "hour had come" (John 13:1 ESV) the Son courageously went to the cross to keep the promise of the Father. When the Spirit of God lifted the Son from His grave, the Holy Spirit then went into the world to continue the ministry of the Son.

The Three Persons of the Trinity are distinct and unique. Each has His own personality and role in the salvation of the world. They work together selflessly; Each points to the work of the other to "draw all men" (John 12:32) out of sin and death into the light and life of salvation.

When it thunders, hear God say, "This is my beloved Son, with whom I am well pleased" (Matthew 17:5 ESV). And when lightning splits the sky, remember that the "curtain of the temple was torn in two" (Matthew 27:51) so that mankind may enter the presence of God. And when the rain falls, it reminds us that God's grace falls down upon us through the Holy Spirit.

Experience God's comfort and assurance in a thunderstorm.

{ 9 }

Rags and Riches

My daughter is acquainted with Illinois State University football player Colton Underwood, whom she admires very much. Now my daughter does not understand the intricacies of football, but as an athlete herself, she could tell that Underwood's athleticism made him an asset to the team. By watching him play throughout the season, she noticed he was quicker, stronger and more adept at his position than his opponents. Her assessment of him proved to be accurate: He signed a contract to play professional football.

In his college career this defensive end earned many personal achievements, but the program itself was not one of the rich and famous in college athletics. He didn't play for a national championship. There were no conference or division titles. Yet, by the time the draft ended, this young man had signed as a free agent.

Most of us appreciate rags-to-riches stories. Stories of average or downtrodden people who rise above circumstances to overcome in the world resonate in all of us. They are stories of hope. And we all hope to be holding on to life's pendulum when it swings upward.

Here is the metaphor:

Jesus Christ's life is the greatest rags-to-riches story ever told. He worked briefly as a carpenter until He left home to be an itinerant preacher. Once He left His parents' home, He was often homeless. He wandered through this world in the company of twelve men, living on the charity of others. His revolutionary message of God's love and salvation, which threatened the power of sinful religious leaders, provoked His enemies to have Him nailed to a cross. All of His life seemed a failure. However, that is not the end of the story.

God the Father did not leave His Son a pauper. Through the cross came the riches. Through His unfathomable power and might God raised Jesus from the dead. The author of the book of Hebrews wrote, "Let us fix our eyes on Jesus, the author and perfecter of our faith, who for the joy set before Him endured the cross, scorning its shame, and sat down at the right hand of the throne of God" (12:2).

Sin has made us spiritual paupers and has clothed us in the rags of rebellion. Still God has ensured that we can rise above our spiritual destitution by believing in Christ's atoning work on the cross. Because Christ has passed through the indignity of sin and death into glory, He offers us safe passage through "the valley of the shadow of death" (Psalm 23:4 ESV) so that by faith we can take our rightful place as a royal citizen of God's kingdom. When by faith we pass through the indignity of the cross with Christ, then His rags-to-riches story becomes our own. "For He called you to share in His Kingdom and glory" (1 Thessalonians 2:12 NLT).

{ 10 }

The Dinner Table

When I was growing up, my mom served dinner each evening promptly at 5:30, when Dad arrived home from work. Just prior to his arrival, friends were sent home; homework was set aside; the TV was turned off; the house was picked up; and hands were washed. When the family gathered at the table, it was a special time for us to be alone together.

Since we had been separated by daily demands, the table was the place to catch up on one another's day. Dad's work stories kept me enthralled. Listening to him talk with Mom made me feel important and included in their world.

Other times, my parents listened as we vented our frustrations or concerns about school, classmates, or neighborhood scuffles. Sometimes they refereed the arguments among us three girls. Bickering, laughter, and conversation seasoned our

family's time together, as we shut out the world and recon-
nected as a family.

Here's the metaphor:

We Christians spend most of our time running and playing
in the secular world. Our lives are crammed with activities. We
race here and there, rarely slowing down for time to reflect, that
is, not until we hear Jesus say, "Here I am! I stand at the door
and knock. If anyone hears My voice and opens the door, I will
come in and eat with him, and he with Me" (Revelation 3:20).

During His incarnation Jesus sat at tables and shared meals
with many people. Salvation was the dinner discussion between
Jesus and Zacchaeus. While resting at a well with a Samaritan
woman, He engaged her in conversation about Living Water.
He provided food for more than five thousand people so He
could teach the crowd about the Bread of Life from heaven. He
ate with sinners, and He fed them with His divine mercy and
compassion along with their dinner.

Guests listening at the meal in Bethany might have heard
Lazarus, his sisters, and Jesus discuss life, death and resurrection. That conversation extended into a public discourse when
Jesus comforted Martha with His words after Lazarus' death,
"Your brother will rise again" (John 11:23). To which she re-
plied, "I know he will rise again in the resurrection at the last
day" (John 11:24). And at the most important meal in history,
the night before His crucifixion, Jesus gathered His disciples
into the upper room, shut out the world, and taught them the
meaning of the coming hours. He reminded them, "You heard
Me say, 'I am going away and I am coming back to you.' If you

loved Me, you would be glad that I am going to the Father, for the Father is greater than I. I have told you now before it happens, so that when it does happen you will believe" (John 14:28-29).

Come in from the world and join Christ at God's family communion table. Jesus' presence meets us at the table to open our hearts and minds to the Scriptures' teachings about God, sin, salvation, and eternal life. At the table the Holy Spirit illuminates our souls with the truth of Christ's life, death and resurrection.

Jesus invites us all to come to the table and eat the Bread of Life, drink the cup of salvation, and share communion with our God.

{ 11 }

Bitter Waters

Recent downpours have left standing water on the ground. Out in the fields it pools between the rows of corn and soybeans. In low lying places, greater amounts of rain water have collected. One stagnant pool has filled the air with the stench of rotting plants, souring soil and decomposing earth. Without movement, water turns putrid.

Yet flowing water has a way of cleansing the earth, to make everything smell fresh with life, like a rushing stream bursting forth after an early spring rain.

Here's the metaphor:

Sin is the stagnant water of our spiritual life. It pools in our souls, lifting the offensive odor of death into the nostrils of God. This is what the Psalmist wrote: "See if there is any offensive way in me, and lead me in the way everlasting" (Psalm

139:24). The Psalmist prayed that God would uncover the standing water of sin that was decaying his soul and remove it.

At the cross God in Christ expunged the offensive odor of sin. On the cross, Christ submerged His perfect soul into the fetid, foul, filthy standing water of sin. Once the wooden cross touched the "bitter water" (Numbers 5:23) of sin, "the water became sweet" (Exodus 15:25 ESV). Through His sacrifice, the "living water" (John 4:10) of the Holy Spirit washed away the stench of death and brought new life to our souls.

Believers are invited to kneel at the cross and let Christ's Holy Spirit go down into the polluted pool of sin in their souls and "stir up the waters" (John 5:4). These living waters flow into our souls, wind their way through our thoughts and flood our hearts with the headwaters of heaven. "…the river of the water of life, [is] as clear as crystal, flowing from the throne of God and of the Lamb down the middle of the great street of the [heavenly] city" (Revelation 22:1-2).

When the "bitter water" of our sin is touched by the splintered, bloodstained wood of Christ's cross, they are purified into sweet living water for our thirsty souls.

{ 12 }

Hands

Do we really ever reflect on the marvel of our hands? We use them all day long, but, since so much of what we do with them is reflexive or automatic, we rarely think about them. We wave, grasp a glass, use a fork or wash a dish. They are instruments of creativity: We make supper, mud pies or pottery without giving a thought to their involvement in the action. Hands catch a baseball, play instruments and grip paint brushes. Our hands can hold a book, a remote or a baby and type on a keyboard, sometimes all at once. Our hands are reliable and ready, constantly working. Still how we use our hands reveals something about our character. If we are openhanded with what we have, others see our generosity and hospitality. However, if we keep them closed or tightly fisted, they can depict hostility.

Here's the metaphor:

When Christ walked among us, the way in which He used His hands not only revealed His human nature but they also pointed us to His divine character. As Mary and Joseph's son, His hands, like ours, were working constantly. He used His hands to attend to His ordinary daily tasks, such as gathering wood, carrying jugs or using tools. He wrote in the dirt, broke bread and poured wine. We assume that He used them as we do with our loved ones: He held His mother's hand, picked her flowers and gave her a hug. He played with His siblings, helped His friends and worked with Joseph. His hands were those of a man.

Beyond that, though, His hands were also the hands of God. Using His hands, Jesus healed the blind, the lame and the sick. He raised the dead and He fed the masses, and He clutched His hands in prayer. His were the hands that separated the "water under the expanse from the water above it" (Genesis 1:7). His hands "formed the man from the dust of the ground" (Genesis 2:7). His hands were God-strong: They held back the waters so the Israelites could cross on dry land. They held the sun in place until Joshua secured victory. His were the palms of eternal God.

And when the soldiers drove the nails into the hands of Jesus the man, the hands of God endured the agony and, out of love for us, secured our salvation. These mighty hands of God in Christ broke the chains of sin, overpowered death and pushed down the gates of hell. And, in conquest, He raised victorious hands to God, and He was lifted into heaven.

In the hands of Christ, God has achieved His purpose, "so that people may see and know, may consider and understand, that the hand of the Lord has done this…" (Isaiah 41:20).

{ 13 }

Cleaning Closets

My daughter is cleaning her closet. I know I should be thrilled, except that her process usually leaves a mess in the upstairs hallway in front of my office door. Currently, just across the office threshold is one large garbage bag filled with stuffed animals, a medium-sized box of DVD's, three boxes full of shoes and five additional boxes—contents unknown.

My daughter cleans as many of us probably do, in stages: First, she decides to clean. Next, everything in the closet must be pulled, pushed or dragged out and made into a big messy pile in the middle of the room. She then enters the sorting phase: Broken, faded, ripped or out-of-style items get tossed. Items that are still in good condition but are no longer being used find their way to the hallway, and they are marked as donations. At last, she returns the remaining items to the closet.

Here's the metaphor:

Our heart, mind and soul need spiritual cleaning. Accumulating spiritual junk comes easily to us. Anger gets trapped in our hearts, and ugly thoughts hide in the recesses of our mind. Hurtful words become squatters in our souls and build fires of resentment.

Eventually, this spiritual junk presses against our spiritual closet doors and bursts forth into our lives as ungodly behaviors and rebellious actions. Our first instinct is to barricade the mess inside. But this sinfulness won't go away until we purge it, and the process of cleaning takes place.

We need to follow King David's example and ask God to "create in me a clean heart, O God, and renew a right spirit within me" (Psalm 51:10 ESV).

What does this process look like? First, we need to confess, which means that we must admit that our sinful nature is in need of Christ's cleansing. Next, we open our heart, mind and soul to the conviction of the Lord's powerful Spirit: He will push, pull and drag everything ungodly out and make a big messy pile.

As we see the mounting clutter of corruption, we are moved to repent and to ask Christ to carry the sinful debris to the cross. As the rubble of rebellion dwindles, we rejoice in God's forgiveness. Then the Spirit mends the broken dreams, shattered hopes and crushing sorrow caused by sin, and then He centers us on the presence of God. Finally our heart, mind and soul are renewed in Christ, and our relationship with God is restored through the Spirit.

"Rid yourselves of all the offenses you have committed, and get a new heart and a new spirit" (Ezekiel 18:31). Let's get cleaning!

{ 14 }

Empathy

My children insist that I do not understand their circumstances in life. "You don't understand" is their mantra, and they use it in an attempt to convince me that I should accept their misguided plans. Even when I give them examples from my life that confirm my understanding of their situations, they can't recognize their significance. In their minds, I still don't understand.

They forget that I grew up once. They are certain that I have never gone through school. In their minds, I have never said goodbye to friends and moved, retired from a sport or had a job. They question whether I have ever known the turmoil of transition or the stress of decision making. They think I know nothing about paying bills, finding housing or planning for the future. My wonderful children are so blinded by their inexperience and arrogance that they fail to recognize that not only have

I gone through all the things they are facing but also that I am still going through many of them.

Here is the metaphor.

Every day, we tell God that He doesn't understand our circumstances. We insist that He can't understand the world because He is up there, on a throne, out of the fray. We tell Him how much He doesn't understand about our life. We think He knows nothing about sorrow, pain or death. And we are certain that He doesn't realize how difficult it is to battle sin, fight temptation or live lawfully. We persist in the argument that He doesn't understand for one reason: so we can determine the course of our lives, no matter how misguided our plans.

Yet we have proof in His Word that God understands our circumstances. To demonstrate His empathy with our predicament, the Son of Man came down to earth. God came down from the place of perfection and became a man so He could endure the hardships of earthly life.

He spent forty days in the desert tempted by Satan, said goodbye to His friends in the Upper Room at the Last Supper and then carried our sins to the cross. When the nails of iniquity pierced His hands, grief pierced His heart. When the spear of transgression slashed His side, sin slashed His perfect soul. When the shroud of death covered His physical body, and His time on earth ended, He was separated from His loved ones. And as the shroud of death draped His divine nature He anguished with separation from God.

Our Savior became a man so He could participate in the human experience. Not only does He understand our plight, He took our punishment and atoned for the wages of our sin, which cause us all that pain and suffering.

The next time we insist that God doesn't understand our plight, remember that Jesus was a man on earth. He was like us in all the human ways. "For we do not have a high priest who is unable to sympathize with our weaknesses, but one who in every respect has been tempted as we are, yet without sin" (Hebrews 4:15 ESV).

{ 15 }

Discipline

Recently my daughter had a disappointing week. A string of unfortunate events dashed her dreams of moving to another state. I listened as she described her vision of a tarnished future. In spite of her trampled hope, she has begun to regroup, assess the damage and consider how to salvage relocation to a warmer climate.

As I listened, she picked through the rubble of her dreams to find the pieces she could use to move forward. The conversation brought clarity. She realized that if she wanted to move, she needed to finish her college degree and find a job that pays beyond minimum wage. During what seemed like a setback, she could see an opportunity to save money and secure funds for her departure.

Meeting these goals will mean making changes. More time will go to studies instead of play. Money will have to flow into a savings account instead of coffee shops or concert tickets or restaurants. Overall, she needs to apply discipline to her life to achieve her goals.

Here's the metaphor:

Sin tarnished our future and trampled on our hope of eternal life. Disobedience derailed the dream of dwelling forever in the everlasting house of the Lord. To help us realize our dream of eternity, the Holy Spirit applies divine discipline to our corrupt nature. The Lord's discipline brings life and health to our sin-damaged souls. "Lord, your discipline is good, for it leads to life and health" (Isaiah 38:16 NLT).

Our unruly nature is determined to violate God's commands and pull us away from Him. Without divine discipline from the Holy Spirit, our souls are set adrift in the sea of sin and perish in death. The human will alone is too weak to subdue the enemy of our souls or our sinful nature. A loving God designed a plan of assisted living. He sent His Son into the world to overpower sin at the cross and then gave us His almighty Spirit so we can lead disciplined, obedient lives in His strength.

The Spirit abides in us to expose our waywardness and to incite in us the desire to live under divine authority, where we grow in wisdom and love for Him. Only the Spirit can conform our thoughts and actions to the holy standards of God. Paul wrote, "For God did not give us a Spirit of timidity, but a Spirit of power, of love and of self-discipline" (2 Timothy 1:7).

Opening our lives to the discipline of the Holy Spirit allows our thoughts and actions to align with the thoughts and actions of God in Christ. As the Spirit corrects our ways and transforms our behavior, we are able to meet our spiritual goal, "to serve [God] without fear in holiness and righteousness . . . all our days" (Luke 1:74-75).

{ 16 }

Looters

Inevitably, riots spawn looting, as the scenes from those in Ferguson, Missouri, proved recently. The news broadcasts were filled with images of area stores that had been vandalized and looted during the disorder. People who had little to do with the peaceful protests took the opportunity to foment the unrest for their gain. Windows were smashed. Mobs pillaged and plundered businesses until all merchandise vanished.

During riots such as these, police forces are stretched thin, trying to maintain order, which leaves the local merchants vulnerable to looters. Outnumbered by marauders, without police protection, the stores are susceptible to theft.

Here's the metaphor.

The world is full of spiritual looters. Unbelievers, "false teachers" and "false prophets" (2 Peter 2:1), know when the mind is stretched thin and preoccupied by disease, grief, trouble and distress; they swoop upon the hurting soul. While our minds are distracted by the difficulties we face, these looters can lead us away from God. They pillage and plunder the soul with persistent attempts to steal the truth with "destructive heresies" (2 Peter 2:1), snatch faith by "denying the sovereign Lord" (2 Peter 2:1), mock God and lead the vulnerable away from the Lord's presence with "stories they have made up." (2 Peter 2:3).

Jesus prayed that His disciples would not become victims of looters. The night before His crucifixion, He prayed, "Holy Father, protect them by the power of your name" (John 17:11). He knew that His death would occupy their minds, making them vulnerable to the looters, who would deny God's work of redemption, sneer at salvation and dismiss the resurrection. Jesus prayed that the divine nature of God would protect their hearts and wrap their minds in truth.

When people hurt, we are called to pray for God's protection to surround and strengthen their souls. Through intercession we ask the Holy Spirit to bind our prayers to Christ's prayers, so the weak are not victimized by spiritual looters. We ask, with certainty, for God to clothe the vulnerable soul with the "full armor of God" (Ephesians 6:13). We pray alongside Jesus, beseeching God to surround the anemic soul with the "belt of truth...the breastplate of righteousness...the shield of faith...the helmet of salvation...and the sword of the Spirit, which is the word of God." (Ephesians 6:14-17).

"I urge you, first of all, to pray for all people. Ask God to help them; intercede on their behalf, and give thanks for them" (1Timothy 2:1 NLT).

{ 17 }

Solitude and Silence

Sunday mornings are typically very quiet on the bike trail. This one was particularly still. Fishermen were absent from Pierce Lake. I didn't spot a biker, runner or walker on the path, in the park or on neighborhood streets. I was alone.

Solitude is something I appreciate; however, it felt strange not saying good morning to the regulars who share the path with me on most Sunday mornings. On those days, we exchange waves and nod in greeting. We slip in a quick "hello" and "have a good day" as we pass. With these gestures and salutations we acknowledge one another's commitment to exercise, and we respect the dedication that brings us to the trail at dawn. These verbal expressions and waves are signs of support and encouragement; they are ways of applauding our devotion to health and well-being. We are united by our dedication to strengthening our bodies.

Here's the metaphor:

Christians often travel alone. We nod to other worshippers. We share a smile and a hand shake during the passing of the peace in church. At coffee hour we mingle, talking about our children's sporting events or school activities. Sometimes we connect with fellow pet owners, or swap Pinterest recipes and videos we've seen on Facebook. But when it comes to conversations about faith and belief, we are silent. Rarely is a spiritual topic broached.

When no one talks about spiritual matters, we wonder whether our spirit matters.

The most vital aspect of the Christian faith is fellowship— fellowship with our glorious Lord and with His people. John says, "We proclaim to you what we have seen and heard, so that you also may have fellowship with us" (1 John 1:3).

Talking about Jesus Christ is entering into communion with Him and uniting with His faithful community. Gathering together strengthens our faith and knowledge. We bond in the Spirit through discussions about Scripture. When the faithful gather for prayer, the community is encouraged by our Lord's answers. We witness as one body the power of our Lord responding to our supplications and petitions. Encouragement comes through communion, as we confess our sins, remember our Savior's sacrifice and receive forgiveness and grace from God. As we worship together in Spirit and truth, we grow together in good spiritual health.

God calls us to fellowship with Him so the Spirit can unite believers with believers to make one strong, faithful and healthy body of Christ.

"Let us not give up meeting together, as some are in the habit of doing, but let us encourage one another—and all the more as you see the Day approaching" (Hebrews 10:25).

{ 18 }

The Domino Effect

Here are a few things I have learned while fasting from television. When the TV is off, my productivity and energy levels go up. Creativity makes its way into my day. I do more of what I like and what I need to do: reading, writing, cooking, cleaning, and even laundry. The moments that I formerly spent watching images flicker on the screen have now been rededicated to my real friends and family.

Watching television dwindled away my precious time. One show led to another and another. Several hours would pass, and still I surfed the air waves for another show or movie. Television is deceitful: It makes me believe I am actually doing something. But really I'm not. Watching television is passive not active. Television needs only electrical power, not human participation. It separated me from the people who were most important to me.

Food has been given its rightful place. If I'm hungry, I eat. Too often I had been using food as a condiment to programming. Viewing countless hours of food ads encouraged me to consume countless calories of snacks and treats.

Basically, I had made viewing television a bad habit, one that made me physically lazy. One bad physical habit started a chain reaction of other bad habits: overeating, wasting time, slothfulness, and so on.

Here's the metaphor:

One bad spiritual habit can create a domino effect of bad habits that make us spiritually lazy.

Our souls suffer the consequences of our bad spiritual habits. Our first bad habit is setting our spiritual standards using a worldly model. For example, the world likes to stay up late. If Christians consistently stay up late we oversleep, which leads to a loss of prayer time. A loss of prayer time can lead to other bad spiritual habits that rob us of our connection to God.

Feasting on anything that the world offers up can separate us from Jesus Christ. For instance, reading worldly authors, but not God's Word or books by godly writers, can weaken our souls. Becoming enthralled with secular philosophers who expound on the virtues of man, but deny God's power, can turn us from the truth and cause us to doubt Him. We listen to secular music, but not sacred music, which gives us theological insights about the truths of God.

While not sinful in themselves, these pursuits can distract us from what our souls crave: daily time in Scripture, which expounds on the virtues of one man, Jesus Christ our Savior.

The world is deceitful. It keeps us busy running around, often without good reason, while convincing us that such a haggard lifestyle is pleasing to God. Caution: Running around in the world is not the same as participating in the life of God. Sitting at Jesus' feet, kneeling in prayer and being still are participating in the life of God.

If we accept the premise that one bad habit promotes other bad habits, then, perhaps, the reverse might also be true: A good habit promotes other good habits. Only by the power of the Holy Spirit can we form good spiritual habits. Cultivating these spiritual habits can lead to the health of our souls, stronger faith, and deeper participation in the life of God.

Our good spiritual habits begin when we "draw near to God with a sincere heart in full assurance of faith . . . " (Hebrews 10:22). Work to develop good spiritual habits in your life.

{ 19 }

The Offensive Line

Yesterday, the Dallas Cowboys beat the Seattle Sea-hawks—thanks to the Cowboys' big, quick, strong offensive line. The line protected quarterback Tony Romo, giving him plenty of time to run plays. Later, a weak, slow, ineffective Giants offensive line left quarterback Eli Manning vulnerable and unprotected. The Giants lost.

Here's the metaphor:

In our spiritual lives we try to build our own offensive line to protect ourselves against sin. It is a weak, feeble line that cannot stand against sin. It is a line of denial. Instead of admitting sin, we rationalize it and define sin from our human perspective not God's. We compare ourselves to others, not to our impossibly high standard, Jesus Christ. We water down the truth and call sin a "mistake." We decide sin is no big deal to God because He loves us. We accept no responsibility for our wrongdoing. And we disclaim that our sinful nature is an affront to God. This man-made offensive line is weak and useless and leaves us vulnerable to sin and the workings of Satan.

God, however, has put together a very strong offensive line against sin: The Father, Son and Spirit all work together to conquer sin and transform our sinful nature into its perfect, original condition.

The Spirit convicts us "of guilt in regard to sin" (John 16:8). It is the job of the Spirit to awaken us from our fallen and corrupt state. He does this by speaking the truth to us; "the sinful mind is hostile to God" (Romans 8:7). He shows us that our sinful nature makes us enemies of God. Our sinful nature is consistent with the will of Satan, not the will of God. When sin rules our lives then our will is bent on the ruination of God. By God's great mercy and grace, He sends His Spirit to regenerate our lives and redirect us from the path of sin that leads to death and destruction to the path of righteousness, which leads to life.

The offensive line of God stands strong at the cross, where the Spirit opens our minds to God's mercy and salvation. The Son carries our sin to the cross so God's wrath can attack and destroy it. Jesus battled sin and its purveyor, Satan. He endured God's assault against sin. He survived Satan's arsenal of weapons unleashed against Him. He fought sin and death to save us, while we were "yet sinners" (Romans 5:8 KJV) fighting against Him.

When the Son died, sin and Satan appeared victorious.

But God's judgment on Satan, "the prince of this world" (John 12:31), was just beginning. When the Father saw the body of His Son in the depths of Sheol, He condemned "the prince." The righteousness of the Son burst forth in the darkness of Hades and lawlessness, and rebellion and sin were conquered. "The gates of hell," Satan's offensive line, could "not prevail against" (Matthew 16:18 KJV) the Righteous Son. The Son rose triumphant.

"Through faith you are being protected by God's power for a salvation that is ready to be revealed . . ." (1 Peter 1:5 ISV).

This is God's offensive line!

{ 20 }

Facing the Headwind

My legs pushed vigorously on the bike pedals, making quicker and quicker revolutions. Beating steadily and effortlessly, my heart synchronized with each cycle of the chain as I ascended and descended the hills on my route. I was cruising.

As I rounded the curve to head home, a strong headwind blew me off my rhythm. No longer cruising, I found that my maximum effort produced minimum advance. My legs weakened with fatigue, and even shifting gears failed to bring harmony between me and my tenacious opponent. At last, to find a few moments of rest from the relentless agitator, I zigzagged the rest of the way home.

Here's the metaphor:

God sends His Holy Spirit headlong into our lives. Look at the following examples from Scripture.

A great wind from the Lord ultimately got Jonah tossed into the violent sea and swallowed by the whale.

Moses and the Israelites crossed the Red Sea on dry land when the "Lord drove the sea back with a strong east wind" (Exodus 14:21) so the people could escape the Egyptians.

And Jesus calmed the fears of His disciples by rebuking the winds during a violent squall on the lake.

It was the day of Pentecost when "a sound like the blowing of a violent wind came from heaven," (Acts 2:2) creating the church.

Once the Holy Spirit of God blows into our lives, nothing is the same. Jonah surrendered his personal ambitions for those of God. Moses met the Deliverer, and in spite of Moses' protests, God made him a deliverer. After the winds on the lake had calmed, Jesus' divine nature was revealed. And God showed again His creative side when His Spirit descended on the people and formed the church during Pentecost.

God deliberately sends the headwind of the Holy Spirit into our lives to throw us off our worldly rhythm. He intentionally knocks over our carnal desires, purges us of selfish purposes and topples our ungodly motives.

God sends His holy headwind into our lives to blow away the world, reroute us according to His purpose and fill our souls with the living Christ.

{ 21 }

A Tiny Extravagance

In Mark, Jesus contrasts the parsimony of the rich with the magnanimity of one poor widow: "And he sat down opposite the treasury and watched the people putting money into the offering box. Many rich people put in large sums" (Mark 12:41 ESV). Then with awe, Jesus watched as the poor woman dropped "two very small copper coins," "all she had to live on" (Mark 12:42, 44) into the coffer. Touched by the extravagant gift, He commented, "This poor widow has put in more than all those" (Mark 12:43 ESV).

She gave everything to God.

By that day's monetary standards, those tiny coins were a pittance; however, that pittance represented a total sacrifice on the part of the widow. Once surrendered, that offering became priceless, beyond measure in the Kingdom of God.

Here's the metaphor:

The widow's mite represents Christ's earthly life. For His journey into the world He "made Himself nothing, taking the very nature of a servant" (Philippians 2:7). He gave up His throne in heaven and surrendered His human life to the will of God "to do away with sin by the sacrifice of Himself" (Hebrews 9:26).

By the world's standards, Christ's life, ministry and death were worthless. The world repudiates Jesus. It refuses to acknowledge the significance of His sacrifice on its behalf. In the eyes of the world His earthly contributions were a pittance compared to its money and power. The world watched Him live as a pauper and die as an insurrectionist.

His extravagant gift to God—the giving of His life—"even death on a cross" (Philippians 2:8) was invaluable to the Kingdom. His death purchased our debt. Paul in 2 Corinthians 8:9 sums it up this way, "For you know the grace of our Lord Jesus Christ, that though he was rich, yet for your sake he became poor, so that you through His poverty might become rich."

Jesus gave to the world His mite, but the world did not value it. His life seemed insignificant, yet the world would be saved through it. Consider Christ's gift this way: Coin number one, God becomes poor in earthly flesh. Coin number two, God dies. Study these coins. Stare at the human side, and see Jesus the man of God. Now flip it over and stare at the heavenly side, and let the Spirit reveal Jesus, God of man.

{ 22 }

In the Net

Circulating on Facebook is a short video about a remarkable rescue: While snorkeling, a swimmer happened upon a young female humpback whale lying motionless in the water. He presumed that she was dead, but then he saw her raise her head slightly and force a stream of air through the blowhole.

While swimming around the mammal, the man noticed that the whale's tail and dorsal and pectoral fins were tangled in a fisherman's nylon net, causing the animal's distress. Imagine how that poor whale thrashed and flailed and rolled trying to free itself from its sinewy captor, only to become more and more entangled in the nylon strands until it was near death from exhaustion.

Working quickly, the swimmer and some of his friends used a single knife to cut, hack and pull at the net until the whale broke free. Cheers erupted as the tired rescuers watched the whale swim away.

Moments later, the whale breached the surface in what the deliverers described as a celebration of joy and gratitude: For the next hour the whale showered them with breaches and tail slaps, a full surface display of jubilation.

Here's the metaphor:

Disobedience to God wrapped us in a net of sin and made us captives to death. We also thrashed and flailed and rolled trying to free ourselves from its grip. But our fight against it entangled us further.

God sent His rescuer, Jesus Christ, to carry a cross and die, an act that cut our bonds and freed us from captivity. His work on the cross brought Him close to fainting with exhaustion; however, He did not fail us, "who for the joy [that was] set before Him endured the cross" (Hebrews 12:2). He endured His pain and suffering to slash and cut at the nets of sin that held us in death. He worked in death to give us life. After the exhausting work of severing sin was over, He returned to the Father rejoicing that the captives had been set free.

All of heaven erupted in joy and celebration. The angels sang, "Amen! Praise and glory and wisdom and thanks and honor and power and strength be to our God for ever and ever. Amen" (Revelation 7:12)! God's work in Christ has accomplished freedom for all persons tangled in the net of sin.

Christ has cut away the sinful net of bondage. Offer a dance of joy and a heart full of thanksgiving to God, because we are freed to rejoice and show our love and gratitude for His sacrifice for us.

{ 23 }

Crazy

An Olympic gymnast once explained to me her recipe for success in the sport. "You have to be crazy," she said, "both inside and outside the gym." She went on to say that all her choices—from the skills she chose to the food she ate—had to align with and support her Olympic goal.

Athletes who are working to reach the top of their game, at an elite level of performance, must be consumed with their objective. They obsess about everything: eating, sleeping and training, which most people outside the pursuit view as crazy. These passionate individuals eschew what others view as normal aspects of everyday life—such as fast food, social engagements and late hours—so they can pursue their goals. For these athletes *normal* means discipline, dedication and devotion to the one ambition. These athletes become grounded in undivided commitment to their aspiration.

Here's the metaphor:

Jesus Christ calls His people to focus their lives on a goal that the world views as crazy: to pursue a life of discipleship, in which we give our undivided commitment to Him. To be a disciple of Christ means that we conform our lives to Christ's and to the will of the Father.

When Jesus says to those pursuing discipleship, "Love the Lord your God with all your heart and with all your soul and with all your strength and with all your mind" (Luke 10:27), He expects them to call upon the Holy Spirit to ensure that this transformation can happen. When He tells His disciples to "forgive men when they sin against you" (Matthew 6:14), it is not a suggestion: It is a command that sets His disciples apart from the unforgiving nature of the world. When he insists, "Go now and leave your life of sin" (John 8:11), He is calling the disciples to stop feeding the sinful nature and start nurturing the life of the Spirit residing within.

When disciples continue on with Christ, they look absolutely crazy to the world, because their lives are grounded in undivided devotion to God the Father. Their habits of daily prayer, Scripture reading and worship align with their devotion to God. And everything they think, say and do appears consistent with the thoughts, words and actions of the Lord. The lives of Christ's disciples must be purged of ungodliness by the Holy Spirit, who justifies, sanctifies and purifies them before God.

Discipleship is craziness to the world but perfect sanity to God. Be crazy!

{ 24 }

The Urgent Harvest

It's a busy time on the farms: The corn and soybeans are ready for harvest, and the farmers and laborers race through the fields bringing in the crops. There is a sense of urgency about the harvest. The entire crop needs to be out of the field before it spoils. The combine harvester is at work day and night, until the fields are razed and the grains stored in silos or shipped to market.

Here's the metaphor:

God is always about the harvest. The Father, Son and Spirit are always in the field reaping, threshing and winnowing the souls ripe for harvest in the Kingdom of God.

Jesus told His disciples, "Do you not say, 'Four months more and then the harvest'? I tell you, open your eyes and look at the fields! They are ripe for harvest" (John 4:35). There is a sense of urgency in Jesus' words. As with any harvest, the work in the field must be completed before the crop spoils. Souls that are not brought in at the harvest will wither and fade and perish in the barren fields of the world.

Christ calls His disciples to do the hard work of laboring in prayer for the harvest. Why would he have to remind us of that? Too often in our prayer lives we work for "food that spoils" instead of "food that endures to eternal life" (John 6:27). We unwittingly get caught up in praying for things to happen in this world and spend very little time praying for things to come to eternal fruition. We have to labor against our sinful nature, which seeks constantly to reap worldly desires in our prayer life, instead of tending to the harvest of God's will. We have to do the hard work of praying with God instead of with our emotions, so we don't trample the crops with our bias towards others. We have to guard against judging a soul's worth or failing to pray for souls we have determined are beyond salvation.

Our shallow view is why Jesus told the disciples to "open their eyes." The harvest belongs to God, not us. Jesus calls us to pray that all of His crops are harvested and stored safely in the silos of eternity. He wants no soul to perish in the fields of the world but to live abundantly in the Kingdom. He calls us to join Him in the field and pray to this end. And when our time on earth is over and we all dwell in the eternal Kingdom of God, we will see the fruits of our hard labor in prayer.

{ 25 }

Be Silent and Listen

When our coaching staff needs to communicate with the athletes we put them in what we call *presentation*, which simply means they move to a designated line on the floor and stand tall and silent so they can hear our words.

We pull the gymnasts out of the noise and activity of the gym, so they can hear our words. When they stand quietly, they can listen and understand our directions. Then, when they have received the information, they return to their workouts and carry out the instructions.

Here's the metaphor:

Each week God calls us out of the noise and activity of the world to His sanctuary. The church is a Christian's presentation line. On Sunday morning, we enter worship to hear God in Christ speak to us. He has created this place of worship to pull us in from the noise and activity of the world and enter His presence. God calls us to worship Him so He can calm our fears by showing us who He is. God reveals Himself to us in worship, so we can declare Him in the world.

God desires that we present ourselves to Him, as stated in 1 Samuel 12:16 (HCSB): "Now, therefore, present yourselves and see this great thing the Lord will do before your eyes." God gathers us for worship in the church so we can witness the wonder and majesty of his Name. He calls us out of the din of the world to hear His gentle voice speak the truth about His Son. Through worship he sets us apart from the world, so we can be united to His presence. He then teaches us and sends us into the world with His Holy Spirit to carry out His teachings.

God has given us a protocol for worship: Enter the sanctuary of God in silence, for this is an offering of honor that demonstrates our respect for His greatness. When entering, we call upon the Holy Spirit to still our thoughts, so we are prepared to receive God's Word. Ask the Lord to hush the worries of our hearts and to fill them with His gracious presence. Quietly approach the Savior and ask Him to heal our troubled souls.

In the silence of the sanctuary the splendor and awe of God are revealed. "Be still and know that I am God" (Psalm 46:10).

{ 26 }

Training Daily

Lately, I have been working out at a gym. To make sure I get the most out of each work out, I began to meet with a club trainer to learn how to use the equipment and to design a plan to build my cardio health and strength. We talked about the benefits of each machine and how it would assist me in achieving my goal. This attention to my goal makes my workout plans efficient, because I know which machine works a particular muscle group. After each workout, I leave the gym ready to put my newly strengthened fitness to practical use at home and work.

Here's the metaphor.

I treat my spiritual life as I do my physical life. I train it daily. The Holy Spirit oversees all my training. He designs a plan each day that will improve the condition of my heart towards God and build strength in my faith in Jesus Christ.

He points out my weaknesses and my failings. Once sin is identified, He ushers me to the cross. It is there I must do the heavy lifting of repentance, as Christ removes the weight of sin from my weak shoulders and places it on His own. I hear Him groan and watch Him slump under the load of the burden. My heart breaks at the sight of my Lord bearing my sin. I am weak with despair at the awfulness I have thrust upon the Perfect Savior, and I crumble to my knees. Yet, in love, Christ extends His pierced hands, grasps mine and then speaks: "Your sins are forgiven … rise and walk" (Matthew 9:5 ESV).

My faith is strengthened through His forgiveness, and I rise and walk with the Spirit to the Word of God for additional study. Here He instructs me in the ways of godliness, my area of weakness. Yet, through the power of the Spirit, I walk away from my sinful ways and walk the path of holiness He has laid out before me. By His strength alone I am able to resist temptation and yield instead to the will of God. The more that I rely on the strength of the Spirit the more my faith is made strong.

After each workout, the Spirit and I head into the world to put my faith fitness to practical use in the world.

"I can do all things through Him who strengthens me" (Philippians 4:13).

{ 27 }

The Other Voyagers

The first new car my husband and I bought as a married couple was a light brown Plymouth Voyager. When we purchased it, very few Voyagers were that color, or so we thought. Shortly after the purchase, we visited a large church near our home. After the service ended, we walked through the vast parking lot back to our car. When we found our car and tried to open it, surprisingly, the keys would not work. It took us a few minutes to realize that we were at the wrong van. Scanning the parking lot for our vehicle, we noticed three other light brown Voyagers.

Prior to our purchase, we had not noticed light brown Voyagers because we didn't need to see them. However, once we owned one, we had to notice them.

Here is the metaphor:

On our way in the world, we are slow to notice the suffering of others. However, God wants us to become aware of the trials of others, so he puts us on the road to suffering with Him. Through our own suffering, we begin to empathize with others.

God walks us through the door of suffering and opens our eyes to what's always been there: He shows us the many people wounded and hurt by this world. Suffering is always around us, but we are insensitive to the heartache and pain in others until we experience it ourselves. The Lord places us on the road of suffering to break our heart, so He can use us in His ministry of healing. "I will remove from them their heart of stone and give them a heart of flesh" (Ezekiel 11:19).

Here is how the Lord removes our heart of stone: He teaches us about the greatest suffering, which is His own. He shows us the scars on His hands and feet to remind us of the cost of our salvation. He shows us His back and speaks the words of Isaiah the prophet, "by his wounds we are healed" (53:5d). He points to His side, where he was "pierced for our transgressions..." (53:5a). He talks about His separation from the Father when we hear Him cry out, "My God, My God, why have you forsaken me?" (Psalm 22:1). He overwhelms us with His own pain and suffering until our hearts break.

Then He fills our broken hearts with His compassion, kindness and patience, so we can minister to the suffering. Because of Christ's lessons, our faith grows stronger, and we can gently lift the weak. We can generously apply the balm of the Gospel to the pain of the wounded. And we can patiently wait with the sufferer until God's healing is accomplished.

{ 28 }

Spiritual Flood

In the days of Noah, God sent tremendous rains onto the earth. According to Genesis 7:18, 20, "The waters rose and increased greatly on the earth . . . The waters rose and covered the mountains." Forty days and nights the waters poured from heaven and destroyed everything: wickedness, evil, corruption and violence.

These were days of divine purging, as the sin of the world was washed away in the raging waters of the flood. During this time, God's "heart was filled with pain" (Genesis 6:6), and mankind suffered destruction for his sinful ways.

Here is the metaphor:

In these days after Christ's ascension, the age of the Holy Spirit, we pray that God will burst forth from the heavens and overwhelm the earth with His Spirit, not to destroy the earth but to save it. Believers need to be humble in attitude but bold in prayer, and call upon the Spirit to flood the earth. We should pray that the Holy Spirit will rain down for forty days and nights washing over the earth, sweeping sin away in the currents of Christ's precious blood, until all people are covered in salvation.

What a rain that will be! Mountains of evil and wickedness will be covered by raging rivers and washed away. Violence and corruption will be destroyed as the rolling river of justice and the never-ending stream of righteousness (Amos 5:24) cleanse the earth.

The flood waters of the Spirit will apply divine pressure to calloused hearts until they crack and open to receive salvation and mercy in Christ. Streams of living water will flow through sin-scorched souls to bring healing.

As God poured water on the earth for forty days, so let us call upon Him for forty days to pour His Spirit into the world. Ask in all confidence for the streams of the Spirit to flow abundantly into our lives and the lives of others.

Pray for forty days that we will see God fulfill His promise to Isaiah, "For I will pour water on the thirsty land, and streams on the dry ground; I will pour out my Spirit ..." (Isaiah 44:3).

{ 29 }

Choosing the Man

Making the rounds on Facebook is a video about a man who was accepted by a lion pride. These strong, fearless, majestic beasts behave like domestic cats when he talks to them, pets them and plays with them. It's an impressive sight.

We appreciate watching humans interact with more powerful creatures. A frail human cohabitating with a stronger beast seems astounding. Even more astonishing is that acceptance is exclusively granted by the animal. In this case, the man did not choose the lions; the lions chose the man.

Here's the metaphor:

We find man interacting with nature awe-inspiring, and, yet, we fail to be amazed by God and man in relationship with one another.

It was divine, awesome, omnipotent Almighty God who extended His hand of acceptance to frail, weak, sinful man.

Majestic, glorious, eternal, invisible God designed a plan so He could live together with corrupt, finite, powerless, carnal man. "He chose us in him before the creation of the world to be holy and blameless in his sight. In love he predestined us to be adopted as his sons through Jesus Christ" (Ephesians 1:4-5). Man did not choose God; God chose man.

God's way of entering into relationship with man was to become a man. According to the Ephesian passage, this plan of unity, of union between man and God, was conceived in the Trinity, executed on earth through Jesus Christ, confirmed by His death on the cross and validated through the resurrection.

To guarantee acceptance between sinful man and sinless God, Christ sent His Spirit into the world to change our nature from corrupt to incorruptible, immoral to moral and unrighteous to righteous, so we could abide with holy God.

The astounding truth is that God poured His divine goodness into the man Jesus and chose to dwell with us in this world. Equally astonishing is the truth that divine goodness alone allows man and God to reside together in the everlasting life of the Trinity. "Surely your goodness and love will follow me all the days of my life, and I will dwell in the house of the Lord forever" (Psalm 23:6).

God, by an act of extreme love and goodness, chose the one Man, Jesus, so He could accept all men, now and forever.

{ 30 }

Heavy Lifting

My coworker and I agree that if we are not sweating while we help our gymnasts through the bar rotation we are not working. This event is labor intensive for us, but keeping the athletes' safe is our first priority; our own well-being becomes secondary. Some days we both leave the gym with arms weak and shoulders stiff and sore from the exertion.

Our shoulder muscles do all the heavy lifting. We use them to get under the weight of the athletes, so our arms are strong enough to assist them in their routines.

Here is the metaphor:

When Jesus Christ calls us to deny ourselves and take up our cross and follow Him (Matthew 16:24), He is telling us to put our spiritual shoulders under the cross of another and lift their burden. He calls us to the labor-intensive work of carrying the weight of others' burdens.

We are so driven by our selfish nature that, when we read this verse, we think only about our picking up our own burden, placing it on our shoulders and following Christ. Carrying our own burden is not the same as following Christ. Jesus Christ "carried our sorrows" (Isaiah 53:4). Christ carries us along the path. We are His first priority; His well-being secondary. In turn, Christ expects us to make others' burdens our priority; our own well-being secondary. He does not give us our own burden to carry; He gives us the burden of another to shoulder. Christ places our neighbors' heaviest burden across our shoulders and enables us through the Holy Spirit to bear their cross when they are too frail to carry it. Then, Christ helps us to bear it.

According to Matthew's gospel account, God makes Simon of Cyrene critical to the plan of salvation. As Jesus walked to his crucifixion, he stumbled under the weight of the cross; it was unbearable in His poor physical condition. At that point, the Roman soldiers drafted Simon to carry the cross to Golgotha. This moment is pivotal: the entire plan of salvation rides on Christ's atoning death on the tree. He must not die on the road under the weight of the cross. He must die on the cross so the weight of sin and death will be lifted off the shoulders of humanity.

When we bear another's cross, we are joining the Holy Spirit in the ministry of salvation.

Each day, Jesus calls us to put our shoulder under the cross of others and lift their burdens, through the means of grace that he gives us for strength: prayer, the Word, action and worship.

"Carry each other's burdens and in this way you will fulfill the law of Christ" (Galatians 6:2).

{ 31 }

The Rules

As my children were growing up, we established rules that we expected them to follow inside and outside the house. My husband and I set these rules so our children would grow into responsible, caring adults. By following the rules, our children showed their respect for us, and they learned to respect others.

Here's the metaphor:

God has also established rules He expects His faithful to follow, in time and eternity, so we are fit to live with Him in His heavenly home. He sent Jesus into the world so He could show us that life could be lived by those rules. To help us to conform to his way of obedience, He has given us His Spirit, who gives us the strength and courage to obey.

Here are God's basic rules, His Ten Commandments:

1. "You shall have no other gods before me." God is head of the house; respect that.

2. "You shall not make for yourself an idol..." We should not drag the corrupt clutter of idols, images or false gods into our lives, or His house.

3. "You shall not misuse the name of the Lord your God..." Always pray on the ground of redemption and ask in accordance with the purpose and will of the Father.

4. "Remember the Sabbath." Once a week, take a day for God alone and worship His majesty, glory and splendor.

5. "Honor your mother and father." Honor your parents; in this way you honor God the Father, Son and Spirit, who are your spiritual parents.

6. "You shall not murder." God is the living God. Through prayer, call on God to bring His Spirit into the lives of those around you, so that all can be saved.

7. "You shall not commit adultery." Don't have affairs with other gods; they just mess with your soul.

8. "You shall not steal." Satan stole creation by enticing Adam and Eve to sin against God. Don't entice anyone to sin. Sin steals them away from God; show them the way to God.

9. "You shall not give false testimony against your neighbor." Tell people the truth about Jesus, as it has been told to you in Scripture and through the Holy Spirit.

10. "You shall not covet your neighbor's house..." Be content with what God provides; He gives to each of us according to His plan of salvation in our lives.

Through the power of the Holy Spirit, we can obey God's rules. When we obey them before others, we show the world our respect for God.

{ 32 }

Schedules

This past weekend I visited some very good friends. My time was limited, so I wanted to spend as much of it as I could with the people who mean so very much to me. Everything else was secondary to our getting together.

Good planning, along with my friends' willingness to re-arrange their own schedules, helped us to optimize our time together.

Here's the metaphor:

God rearranged His schedule to make Himself available to the human race. Humanity lost all knowledge of the Person of God when Adam and Eve tasted forbidden fruit. Not wanting us to perish from "lack of knowledge" (Hosea 4:6) about Him, He disrupted eternity and sent His eternal Son into the world as a finite human. "The Word became flesh and made his dwelling among us. We have seen his glory, the glory of the One and

Only Son, who came from the Father full of grace and truth" (John 1:14).

The purpose of the incarnation was to reveal that God is a person; He showed us His nature in the person of Jesus Christ, and He continues to remind us through the work of the Holy Spirit in our lives and in the world.

In fact, God went to great lengths to effect this revelation: He used eternal measures to ensure that all persons would be able to know Him. He moved heaven and earth via the cross of Christ to guarantee that all people would have an opportunity to know Him personally.

He optimized His plan by proclaiming very early on the coming Savior, made known through Moses and the prophets. He waited until the time was full to announce to a young virgin that she would give birth to His Son, and then He lifted His Son high on a cross so that all people, from the beginning to the end of time, would see He was here.

Immortal God became mortal man and "made His dwelling among us" in the person of Jesus Christ, so through that same Person mortal man could spend his immortal days dwelling with God.

God the Son rearranged His schedule and life in eternity to be available to us in human time. Perhaps today would be a good time to rearrange our schedules to be available to Him. Too often, we treat our glorious Lord as an item on a "to do" list and not as a Person with whom we long to spend our time. We cram our lists with worldly chores and think nothing of spiritual pursuits and cultivating our time with Jesus.

Christ set aside everything to be available to us; everything in our day should be secondary to spending time with Him.

{ 33 }

Projects

My husband is handy around the house. When he starts a project, he looks at all the variables and makes a plan. Sometimes the project turns unpredictable: Some tasks look simple, but they turn out to be complicated. Others that look complicated initially are, in the end, simple. Most hassles result from the unforeseen variables, those hiding beneath the surface. A project might then become more difficult. No matter how difficult the project becomes, however, my husband sticks with it until it's done.

Here's the metaphor.

The sin in our lives is God's project. He sent His Son, "the Lamb of God, who takes away the sin of the world!" (John 1:29) He was "pierced for our transgressions, he was crushed for our iniquities..." (Isaiah 53:5). The light of His resurrection shines in the world, but "men loved darkness instead of light because their deeds were evil" (John 3:19). God broke sin so He could fix us. Through the power of the Holy Spirit, God broke our calloused dark hearts of sin and created a new heart through the reconciling work of the Savior.

However, there is unpredictability in the project. Our sinful human nature wants to retain its sinful human nature. This nature opposes and resists the work of God's Holy Spirit. Human nature insists on hiding its sinful deeds in the dark corners of the heart and strikes at God when His light "shines in the darkness" (John 1:5).

Still, God persists. He exposes our deeds and breaks us. He cracks our cold, hard hearts of sin, removes our "heart of stone" and gives us a "heart of flesh" (Ezekiel 11:19) through the power of the Holy Spirit.

God will "see to it...that none of you has a sinful, unbelieving heart that turns away from the living God" (Hebrews 3:12). He is relentless about finishing this project through His Son. The difficulty of the project depends on our willingness to let the Spirit break our hearts and create in us new hearts according to the will and purpose of God.

{ 34 }

The Marked Trail

While hiking yesterday, my daughter Jen and I followed a path that had been beaten down by thousands of hikers. Even though the path was clearly visible, we still used the trail markers as guides to make sure we got back to the car safely.

Many times, popular trails are so beaten down with foot traffic that it is simple to follow the path; however, following the markers is still a good idea, even more so on difficult or challenging trails where the path is less visible. On these trails, markers are essential for keeping a hiker safe. Without these markers, even the most experienced hiker can stray from the trail and become lost or hurt. These signs point the way and guide hikers safely on their trek.

Here is the metaphor:

God has placed several trail markers in the world that point the way to Him, so we do not stray from our path of faith in

Christ. The Gospel of John refers to these trail markers as "miraculous signs," which illuminate the minds of the believers with the truth of God in Christ.

Jesus said, "Unless you people see miraculous signs and wonders, you will never believe" (John 4:48). He also chided them for their insistence that they needed more and more miracles before they would believe.

In performing miracles, Jesus had tried to show them that HE was the one true miraculous sign. The people of Jesus' day, like many of us, also want to see "miraculous signs." Without them, we question God's presence in our lives, because all we can see is the evil, destructive forces in the world. However, we need to look upon Christ as that sign.

So, lest we forget, here are God's "miraculous signs," which all point to His Son, Jesus:

"The Word became flesh and made his dwelling among us" (John 1:14). God, the Almighty God of the universe and Creator of all, became a man, a finite, weak, frail, human being, Jesus Christ. This "miraculous sign" was given to the world so we would know, "Immanuel—which means, 'God with us'" (Matthew 1:23).

"Father forgive them, for they do not know what they are doing" (Luke 23:34). God, immortal, eternal God, dies. The "miraculous sign" of the cross marks our trail to forgiveness for our sins through the atoning sacrifice of Jesus.

The third "miraculous sign" is Christ's resurrection. "Why do you look for the living among the dead? He is not here; he is risen!" (Luke 24:5-6) God is alive. Sin and death have been conquered by Christ and the heavenly realm is open to all who believe.

Lastly, "the Holy Spirit, whom the Father will send in my name, will teach you all things…" (John 14:26). The Spirit of God dwells in us, so we can know Him.

These miraculous signs were given by God, so believers could find the path to His Kingdom and live forever in the presence of our heavenly Father.

ABOUT THE AUTHOR

Denise Larson Cooper has a passion for Christ and sharing His Word. She is an avid walker and spends many hours in the great outdoors admiring God's creation. She also enjoys photography, leads small group Bible studies and invests the Gospel in all she does. Denise graduated with a Masters of Divinity from Asbury Theological Seminary and worked ten years of inner city ministry in Rochester, New York. A wife and mother of two daughters, Denise currently works as a gymnastic coach in Rockford, Illinois.

Readers can follow her on Facebook at Godnesia.